BR Diesel Locomotive Album

ALAN WILLIAMS

LONDON

IAN ALLAN LTD

First Published 1979

ISBN 0 7110 0971 6

Published by Ian Allan Ltd, Shepperton, Surrey, and printed in the United Kingdom by Ian Allan Printing Ltd.

Front Endpaper: BR/Brush Class 56 heavy freight locomotive No 56.001 pictured approaching Skipton on 24 September 1976 with a Sheffield-Appleby test train (see page 91)./*B. Morrison*

Title Page: Going west it may be, but there seems an assured future for the ubiquitous Class 47 for some time to come; a Paddington-Swansea train in the charge of No 1614 awaits the signal to restart from Neath General in August 1972./*C. Gwilliam*

Below: In view of their undoubted supremacy on the East Coast main line until the advent of HSTs, it always seemed a pity that the 'Deltics' were not given more passenger appeal with a special livery. Instead, BR replaced their original, subdued but distinctive two-tone green livery with the unbecoming bland overall blue livery which now afflicts the entire diesel fleet. Thus dressed, No 55.010 *The Kings Own Scottish Borderer* roars south between Thirsk and Sessay with the 08.50 Aberdeen-Kings Cross on 26 August 1975./*J. E. Oxley*

Introduction

Britain's first main line diesel locomotive, LMS No 10000, took to the rails in late 1947 just a few weeks before the 'Big Four' Railway Companies, still reeling from their wartime battering, were Nationalised to become British Railways on 1 January 1948. Designed by the LMS Chief Mechanical Engineer H. G. Ivatt, No 10000, an orthodox 1,600bhp diesel-electric Co-Co, was joined after a few weeks by an identical sister locomotive, No 10001. Thereafter the pair were to be seen at work on a variety of duties, from express passenger to freight, and were widely projected as the brave new image of British Railways. Nor had the LMS been alone in forseeing the internal combustion engine as the motive power of the future; despite the widespread introduction of his novel but successful Pacifics, and his dalliance with the rather less successful steam-powered 'Leader' class locomotives, the Southern Railway CME, Oliver Bulleid, was also working on a project for diesel-electric traction, while over on the Great Western, individualistic as ever, Hawksworth and his team were working with Brown-Boveri in Switzerland on a proposal for a gas-turbine electric locomotive. Bulleid's work eventually appeared in the form of 1Co-Co1 No 10201 in 1951, while Hawksworth's gas-turbine No 18000 began trials as early as 1949.

Thus, when British Railways came

into being on 1 January 1948 it inherited a considerable fund of ideas and enthusiasm for diesel and gas-turbine electric traction, and stood poised to introduce the diesel era to war-torn Europe. But it was not to be; the fortunes of state-owned industries tend to be dictated by national interests, and the newly formed BR was no exception. The abundance of then still relatively cheap home produced coal, the cost of imported oil, and the possible effects of a switch to diesel traction on employment in the mining industry all tilted the argument firmly back to a continuation of the prewar 'steam is cheap' policy, and even as Bulleid's first diesel locomotive, No 10201, appeared in 1951, the first of almost a thousand new British Railways 'Standard' steam engines was turned out and ceremoniously named *Britannia*. Britain, it seemed, had turned its back on the diesel locomotive, and for the next few years the diesel and gas-turbine prototypes continued to work as oddities on a system still dominated by steam.

By the mid-1950s, however, it became obvious that Britain's railways were slipping drastically behind the newly rebuilt modernised European systems, and that 'steam' was no longer the cheap alternative it had once been; suitable coal was becoming more difficult and expensive to obtain, and staff were less prepared to work in the dirty conditions inseparable from steam locomotive operation and maintenance. In 1955, the British Transport Commission revealed a sweeping 'Modernisation Plan' that aimed to do away with steam traction entirely within 15 years, and to replace it with diesel and electric locomotives and multiple units. Work began at once on designs for the first 'pilot scheme' diesel locomotives, the idea being to build a

small number of each of several different designs and to evaluate them in traffic for some time before large-scale production orders were placed. In fact, however, this desirable state of affairs was never achieved, political and other pressures forcing further bulk orders before, in some cases, the prototypes were even finished, let alone tested. Inevitably, as a result of this headlong rush into dieselisation, by the early 1960s British Railways had become the reluctant owners of some none-too-successful diesel types along with, luckily, some rather good ones. It has taken another decade, and the opportunities for rationalisation of the fleet presented by the Beeching closures and their aftermath, for British Rail to arrive at the present position, with most of the black sheep weeded out to leave a reasonably standardised and balanced diesel locomotive fleet.

Of course, with the benefit of hindsight, it can be said that the wholesale switch to dieselisation could have been undertaken in a more orderly way; that more of the highly successful 'Deltics' should have been ordered; that there should have been fewer of the low-powered classes and more of the more powerful units; or that introduction of diesel traction should have been planned on a region-by-region, area-by-area basis, rather than left to happen in a quite piecemeal way. But the lessons appear to have been learnt, and the implications realised, for although the latest diesels on British Rail, the High Speed Trains, appear at first to be multiple-units, in truth the power cars are essentially single-ended, high-speed streamlined diesel locomotives working on exactly the same push-pull basis as the Class 27 locomotives on the Glasgow and Dundee services out of Edinburgh, the two 2,250hp units providing together an unprecedented 4,500hp per train.

And no longer are diesels introduced on a piecemeal basis, with inadequate servicing facilities; the introduction of the HSTs has been carefully planned on a service-by-service basis, and special maintenance facilities have been provided at the major termini.

For other work, the new 3,500hp 85mph 126ton Class 56 locomotives, based on the successful and popular Class 47 and intended as the future standard heavy freight and mixed traffic type, afford an interesting comparison with the much lighter, less powerful locomotives for similar duties of the late 1950s.

Thus, in just 30 years, and despite many setbacks, main line diesel traction in Britain has passed from its infancy to world leadership in the form of the High Speed Train. This book attempts to briefly record its often chequered but always fascinating progress over these past three decades.

10000

ROYAL SCOT
10001

At first, the Ivatt and Bulleid prototypes were put to work on a variety of passenger and freight workings over the metals of their parent companies, so whilst the two Ivatt LMS 1,600hp Co-Co 'twins' Nos 10000/1 growled to and fro between Euston and Glasgow, usually in tandem and often on the 'Royal Scot,' as in the view of the up train passing Tring **(below left)** on 20 July 1950, the slightly larger 1,750hp Southern prototypes, Nos 10201/2 were undergoing trials on a variety of work on the Southern Region, including the 'Atlantic Coast Express' from Waterloo to Exeter, and the 'Golden Arrow' from Victoria to Dover, on which latter working No 10202 is pictured climbing away from Victoria **(preceding page)** on 10 February 1954. Interestingly, at this time the full day's duty for No 10202 involved two round trips to Dover and back hauling both the 'Golden Arrow' Pullman and 'Night Ferry' sleeping car trains in both directions.

After a few years it was decided to concentrate both the LMS and SR prototypes together for convenience of maintenance and to allow direct comparison of the two designs. At first, the LMS twins came south to join the Southern locomotives, and hence No 10000 was to be seen passing the signal works at Wimbledon **(left)** at the head of the down 'Royal Wessex' on a dull day in 1954, but by 1956 the entire fleet had been transferred to the London Midland Region, where they stayed until their sudden, simultaneous demise in the mid-1960s. By this time they had all acquired the trappings of the BR diesel era, with yellow warning panels and their own special red diamond (Nos 10000/1) or red and white square (Nos 10201/2) coupling codes, although surprisingly No 10001, posing **(below)** alongside a pair of Derby Sulzer Class 24 Bo-Bos in the roundhouse at Willesden on 12 September 1964, still sports its original distinctive waist-level band and raised numerals, plus its steam age Class '5' motive power classification.
/British Rail (2); R. Russell; R. C. Riley

In 1954, the two Southern prototype locomotives were joined by an outwardly similar but more powerful sister, No 10203. Like the existing LMS and SR locomotives, the newcomer was powered by a single 16-cylinder English Electric engine, but pressed to 2,000hp and fitted with a new type of electro-pneumatic control gear which proved to be the prototype for many of the first generation of Modernisation Plan diesels. No 10203 is pictured **(above)** on test at Tunbridge Wells West shortly after introduction on 13 April 1954, sporting the original black livery with silver waistband and numbers but like its sister No 10201, seen **(left)** at Wellingborough on 15 September 1956 on the first day of trials between Derby and St Pancras, it soon acquired the more pleasing lined green steam locomotive livery. Although, like their LMS sisters, the first two SR locomotives could work in multiple, they were not originally built with gangway doors in the centre of the cab to permit access between locomotives when working in tandem, and one of the less pleasing results of their redeployment on the London Midland Region was the fitting of the ugly end doors seen on No 10202 **(below)** as it pulls away from Crewe with a Saturday Euston-bound up express on 21 July 1962. */G. W. Morrison; A.T. H. Tayler; B.A. Haresnape*

10800

10800
RESEARCH LOCOMOTIVE

In addition to his famous 'twins' Nos 10000/1, Ivatt also designed two less-well known mixed traffic main line diesels for evaluation, one diesel-electric, the other diesel-mechanical. The diesel-electric prototype No 10800 was built by North British and turned out in 1950. Looking like a stretched diesel shunter, with its single cab and long 'bonnet' **(above left)** No 10800 had BTH equipment and a single 827hp engine powering its four axles, and was given a 3MT motive power rating. In many ways it could be said to have been the forerunner of the very similar North British Type 1 Bo-Bos introduced in 1958 (see page 18), but about the time these locomotives were beginning to appear, 10800 disappeared into the Brush works at Loughborough, to appear later as their 'Hawk' research locomotive, but still carrying its original number **(below left)** despite quite considerable modification.

The diesel-mechanical prototype, introduced in 1951, was a 2,000hp design built under Ivatt's direction by the Fell Locomotive Co. The 4ft 3in driving wheels, with their massive counterbalance weights, were all originally coupled to give a 4-8-4 wheel arrangement, but by the time the locomotive was pictured at Derby **(above)** in April 1955, the centre section of the rodding had been removed to give, in effect, a 4-4-4-4. No 10100 spent most of its career on mixed traffic duties on the Midland line until its demise in 1957 saw the end of diesel-mechanical traction for other than shunting work. */D.H. Burgess; Brush; P.H. Groom*

523

While the LMS and Southern pursued development of orthodox diesel-electric traction, the Great Western, always different, opted to explore the less charted fields of gas-turbine electric traction. Their first prototype, No 18000, seen leaving Paddington for Plymouth **(above)** in the early 1950s, was an A1A-A1A wheel arrangement design built by the Swiss Locomotive & Machine Works at Winterthur in 1949 and powered by a Brown-Boveri 2,500hp gas-turbine. It was followed in 1951 by No 18100 **(above left)**, a somewhat uglier Co-Co locomotive designed by Hawksworth, built by Metropolitan-Vickers and fitted with a similarly rated gas-turbine. Although they performed with varying degrees of reliability on the Western Region for several years, British Railways did not pursue the development of gas-turbine traction at this stage, and No 18100 was converted to 25kV ac prototype electric locomotive No E2001 in 1958, while No 18000 was withdrawn a little later and subsequently sold back to Switzerland for experimental work. But that was not quite all. Gas-turbine power had one more fling in the early 1960s in the rather surprising form of GT3, seen **(below left)** descending Shap Bank near Greenholme on 19 October 1961 whilst on test shortly after introduction. Powered by an English Electric 2,750hp gas-turbine, GT3 was built on a spare set of BR Standard Class 5 frames and employed mechanical transmission to its 5ft 9in driving wheels through a gearbox and flexible drive. It seemed to the bystander to perform well, and its streamlined steam locomotive-style profile drew admiring glances from the public, but for a number of reasons it did not fit BRs requirements in the mid-1960s, and it is seen stripped **(below)** leaving the Vulcan Works of English Electric for scrap at Salford on 25 February 1966 behind, ironically, a BR Standard steam locomotive.
/E. Treacy; A.R. Carpenter; D. Cross; E.N. Bellass

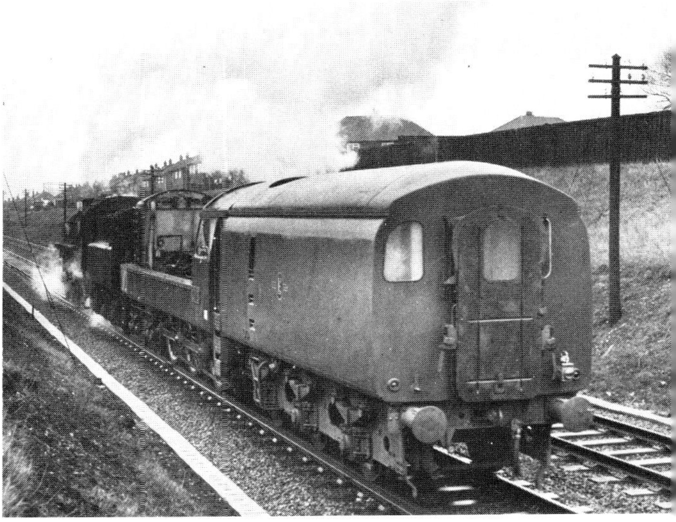

55

All the LMS, SR and GWR prototype diesel and gas turbine locomotives were numbered in the 10000-19999 series of the basic BR steam renumbering scheme adopted after Nationalisation, but with the introduction of the first Modernisation Plan diesels in 1957, an entirely new number series, prefixed 'D' was adopted, which would not only identify the locomotive, but would also indicate its power range. At the same time, each class was also allocated a type number ranging from 1 to 5 according to its power as follows:

Type of Locomotive	*Horsepower*	*Number Range*
1	800-1,000	D8000-D8999
2	1,000-1,450	D5000-D6499
3	1,500-1,750	D6500-D7999
4	2,000-2,750	D1-D1999
5	3,000+	D9000-D9999
Shunter	150-300	D2000-D2999
Shunter	350+	D3000-D4999

Subsequently, however, as a result of alterations to the construction programme, some locomotives were numbered in series outside the group for their type, and thus it was not always possible to ascertain the power of a locomotive solely by its number.

When the last main line steam locomotives were withdrawn in 1968, the 'D' prefix became superfluous and was gradually dropped; at the same time, a new numerical classification code was introduced, based on the power of each class, ranging from 01 for the smallest diesel shunter to 55 for the then most powerful locomotives, the English Electric 'Deltics'. In 1973, British Rail decided to renumber the entire diesel and electric locomotive fleet, using this numerical class code as a two figure prefix to a three figure number, usually commencing at 001 for each class, to identify individual locomotives; sub-classes were numbered in the 100, 200 etc series as necessary.

One of the first classes to transcend the original 1957 numbering scheme was the ill-fated Paxman-engined Class 14 comprising 56 diesel-hydraulic 0-6-0s. These, although of humble Type 1 design of no more than 650hp – little more than a super shunter – were numbered immediately after the Deltics in the D9500-55 series! Even while they were under construction, the yard shunting and short trip freight workings for which they were built was melting away under the combined onslaught of Beeching rationalisation and freight train modernisation which tended towards fully-braked, fixed formation block trains with little use for marshalling yards. Within a few years virtually all wayside station goods yards were closed and torn up, leaving the Class 14s embarrassingly short of work – No D9528 stands idle at Bristol **(below)** on 20 March 1965 – and before long most of the class were in store. Withdrawal began in 1968, when some of the class were barely three years old, and by the end of the following year, the class was extinct as far as BR was concerned, having come and gone in the space of five years. But few of the class were cut up; most were sold to industrial users for further use and many are still in service. Onetime No D9507, now sporting twin headlights at each end but otherwise little changed as British Steel Corporation No 55, waits **(left)** for a fresh load at BSC's Tubes Division Oakley Quarry, near Corby, on 16 November 1975.
/R.A. Panting; K. Lane

D8202

Among the first pilot scheme diesels to appear in 1957 were the first 10 of an eventual class of 44 Type 1, later Class 15, BTH Bo-Bos numbered D8200-43 with Paxman 16-cylinder V-type pressure-charged 800hp engines. Basically 'hood' units with a single double-ended cab amidships, the class were intended primarily for freight work and Nos D8202/3 are seen **(above left)** on such a duty shortly after their introduction. Most of the class spent their time on the Eastern Region in the London Area on inter-Regional and other freight duties; still in green livery, but with yellow ends, D8201 rolls into Kensington Olympia **(below left)** with milk empties from Broad Street on a sunny August day in 1969, while a couple of months later, on 2 October 1969, sister locomotive No D8226, repainted in blue, shunts a mixed rake of freight stock at Liverpool Street **(below)**. Withdrawal began in 1968, and all had gone by the end of 1971, although several members of the class lingered on for a few more years parked in carriage sidings as moblie carriage heating units and renumbered in the Departmental series.
/GEC; J.H. Cooper-Smith; D. Wharton

Also powered by a Paxman 16-cylinder YHXL 800hp engine, but built by North British, were 10 Type 1 Bo-Bos Nos D8400-9 intoduced in 1958. Similar in outline to the Class 15 locomotives, with a single centre cab flanked on either side by full height bonnets, the class spent its 10 years of working life – they were all withdrawn in 1968 – based on the Eastern Region performing similar duties to Class 15. Although withdrawn as the BR numerical classification was introduced, they were allocated Class 16 and the slot has remained vacant since. Clearly illustrating the narrow body and projecting cab arrangement is the view of D8400 standing in the sun **(left)** at Temple Mills in May 1959, while **(below)** sister engine No D8402 scurries off the West London line at Clapham Junction with a short freight from the GE line to Norwood Junction on 30 June 1962.

Perhaps the most attractive of the Type 1 designs were the Clayton Class 17 Bo-Bos, introduced in 1962. Powered again by Paxman but this time with two 6-cylinder 450hp engines, one tucked under each bonnet, they looked set to become the BR Standard type in the power range. But despite their later design, presumably incorporating the lessons learned from the earlier pilot scheme locomotives, it was not to be; although 117 locomotives, Nos D8500-8616, were built – including two, Nos D8586/7, with twin Rolls Royce 8-cylinder 450hp engines – they proved less popular than the earlier types and, suffering from the same disappearing work malaise as the Class 14s,

found themselves slated for early retirement. Many were already in store when withdrawal began in 1968; almost half the class were withdrawn in that year, but then there was a respite for three years, with the numbers in traffic actually increasing at one point as stored locomotives were returned to traffic, until the axe – or rather the cutters torch – fell in the latter half of 1971, and the class disappeared from BR in mid-1972, just a decade after the first locomotive had taken to the rails. But the class is not extinct; although they did not enjoy the wholesale reincarnation of the Class 14s, a few examples found their way into the hands of industrial users, and two, Nos 8521/98, are still used by British Rail for research purposes. Even as ex-works Nos D8559/60 picked their way through Carlisle **(right)** on their way north for service on the Scottish Region, much of the light freight work for which they were intended was disappearing, and as a result the Claytons were often to be seen, coupled in pairs, on rather heavier work. No D8514 leads sister No D8502 as they labour past Greskine on the toil up to Beattock summit **(overleaf)** with a mixed freight on 28 June 1964, while almost exactly four years later, on 13 June 1968, Nos D8538 and D8558, the former in blue livery, the latter in green, climb across moorland on the Benhar branch near Fauldhouse **(below)** with a train of coal from Polkemmet Colliery to the Ravenscraig Steel Works at Motherwell.
/ BR; B. Stephenson; E. Treacy; D. Cross; W.A.C. Smith

Although the first examples of the English Electric Type 1 design were among the earliest pilot scheme diesels to appear in 1957, the class, now BR Class 20, has subsequently enjoyed considerable success as one of the most reliable diesel types on BR, and by a process of elimination now remains as the 'standard' British Rail design in its power range. In contrast to the other Type 1 designs, Class 20 has its single full-width cab at one end, as emphasised in this 1959 view **(below)** of a Class 20 on shed alongside a BTH Class 15 Bo-Bo. Notable for their deep bufferbeams and robust sideframes, construction continued at intervals well into the mid-1960s, English Electric eventually building 228 locomotives in all, Nos D8000-D8199 and D8300-27, all powered by the same EE 8SVT 1,000hp engine. Over the years the class has seen regular duty on the Eastern, London Midland and Scottish Regions, with major concentrations at Immingham, Toton, Tinsley, Eastfield and Haymarket. Still wearing its original green livery, with grey roof, red bufferbeam and the BR coach rather than locomotive emblem, No D8073 rolls downhill **(left)** between Cadder Yard and Bishopbriggs with a Scottish Region freight on 12 May 1962. Because they are essentially freight locomotives and are not therefore fitted with train heating equipment, Class 20s rarely appear on passenger trains, and then only – hopefully – in summer.

One such occasion is depicted here **(above)** as No D8113, deputising for a failed Class 47, hurries the 11.40 Birmingham-Edinburgh through Symington on

10 July 1970. Nowadays, a large number of the class are allocated to Toton shed and, coupled in pairs with the cabs outermost, are the mainstay of Midland line freight activity. One such pairing, Nos 20.180 and 20.140 – the former one of the later members of the class to be fitted with four character headcode panels – picks its way carefully out of Toton yard with an up merry-go-round train **(overleaf)** on 21 November 1977, while a similar pairing of Nos 20.008 and 20.009, both now over 20 years old, waits for signals with an up hopper train at Oakham Crossing **(below left)** on the Midland route via Manton.
/S. Rickard; I. Strachan; B. Chapman; BR; A. Pallet

0 • • 0

2C 90

Regarded by some as 'Baby Warships' because they were both fitted with a single version of the twin NBL/MAN 12-cylinder engines employed in the original North British Warships Nos D600-4, and looked like a stunted version of them, the North British Class 22 B-B locomotives were introduced in 1959 when the Western Region was still resolutely committed to the notion of diesel-hydraulic power for its entire locomotive fleet. The first six locomotives, Nos D6300-5, were fitted with a 1,000hp version of the MAN engine, wired to work in multiple with their five bigger sisters, Nos D600-4, and given a special 'orange square' coupling code; but even before the first example took to the rails, the decision had been taken to build the remainder of the North British 'Warships' to the same design as the Swindon-built 2,200hp B-B versions, and so the remainder of Class 22, Nos D6306-57, were turned out with the single uprated 1,100hp engine and were wired to work with the 'white diamond' D800-series 'Warships'. Doing just this is No D6312 **(below)** as it pilots 'Warship' No D807 *Caradoc* over the summit past Dainton Tunnel signalbox with a heavy down Plymouth train in summer 1960. The novel sideways-folding headcode discs sported by D6312 soon gave way on later locomotives to a standard four-character headcode panel, split on either side of the little-used interconnecting doors, as seen on D6339 **(left)** as it arrives at Torquay on 31 July 1962 with the 11.50 Paignton-Paddington. Despite their reputation for being less than always reliable, and with the trend away from diesel-hydraulic motive power, Class 22 survived well into the 1970s; although the first six 1,000hp locomotives, together with about half of their sisters, followed the first 'Warships' to the breakers in 1968, the remainder, including No D6334 pictured **(above)** rolling into Exeter St Davids from the north with a lightweight milk train on 5 September 1968, survived in traffic for some three more years without further reduction in their numbers, until the entire class was withdrawn over a few months in 1971./*J.K. Morton; M. Pope; J.H. Bird*

Class 22 may have been known by some as 'Baby Warships', but certainly the English Electric Class 23 Bo-Bos were almost universally known as 'Baby Deltics' and the title even enjoyed semi-official status. Introduced in 1959 as part of the original pilot scheme, the 10 Class 23s Nos D5900-9 were equipped with Napier 'Deltic' two stroke pressure-charged engines of 1,100hp derived, like the power plant in the prototype Deltic introduced in 1955, from marine engine practice. From the outset the 'Baby Deltics', which were all allocated to Hornsey (and later Finsbury Park) for Great Northern line outer suburban services, suffered a chequered career; when they were on form, they worked well and put up some sprightly performances for a relatively low-powered Type 2 design, but far too much time was spent on shed or ignominiously parked somewhere 'failed' because of a disturbingly high incidence of crankcase and cylinder fractures, requiring frequent major attention and causing chaos to GN suburban timekeeping. From the summer of 1962, they were gradually withdrawn from traffic until the last succumbed in June 1963, and over the next two years they were modified to give rather more reliable performance. At the same time, the opportunity was taken to remove the rarely, if ever, used end doors and other end clutter, including the original

'folding disc' headcode system, which was replaced with a standard BR four-character headcode panel. The resultant clean-up of the front end was striking, as shown by a comparison of D5901 in original form negotiating the station throat at Kings Cross with an arriving surbuban train on 18 April 1961 **(above left)** and modified sister locomotive No D5909, by now in blue livery, backing down onto a train at the same location on 7 February 1969 **(below left)**. In modified form, the 'Baby Deltics' became the workhorses of the Great Northern; this view of Sunday engineering work in progress at Langley in June 1968 **(above)** reveals three of the class at work, with D5904 in the foreground and D5901 behind on engineers' trains, while sister D5908 runs light in the centre of the scene. Withdrawal began not long after in the autumn of 1963, and by March the following year Nos D5900/3/4/8, along with Class 15 No D8233, were to be seen **(below)** stored out of use at Clarence Yard depot. The last of the class, Nos 5905/9, were withdrawn in July 1971 but No D5901 remained in intermittent use in Departmental stock until the mid-1970s, employed by Derby Works in connection with development work.
/D. Kingston; J.H. Bird; D.L. Percival (2)

BEARSTED
D5002

D5023

Probably among the most successful of the first generation diesels, and certainly the most numerous, the Derby/Beyer-Peacock Sulzer-engined Type 2s are today still to be found at work, in their various forms, quite literally from Wick and Thurso to Plymouth and Penzance.

Introduced in 1958, the first 151 'Derby Sulzers' Nos D5000-D5150 were equipped with that company's 6-cylinder 1,160hp 6LDA28 engine and went to work on the Southern, Eastern and London Midland Regions, although in both of the first two cases as a temporary expedient until more powerful locomotives – Class 33 on the Southern, Class 31 on the Eastern – arrived on the scene. The locomotives allocated to the Southern had the unenviable task of proving themselves to a regime dedicated to electric traction and in the midst of furthering this form of propulsion throughout Kent. They were tolerated rather than welcomed by the Southern men, and it is probably true that the Southern were as pleased to see them go as the London Midland were to have them back. Nevertheless, despite the chauvinism of the Southern men, they did well under the often adverse conditions of electrification work; two, Nos D5012 and D5014, pass through Bearsted **(left)** on a March Sunday in 1959 with a Folkestone-Victoria boat train diverted via the Maidstone loop because of engineering work on the main line. Paradoxically, when the loaned locomotives returned to the London Midland, they again found themselves in the midst of electrification work, but of a rather different kind; beneath newly erected gantries for the southerly extension of the West Coast main line 25kV electrification comes Willesden based D5023 **(below left)** as it pulls away from Tring with the 15.16 Bletchley-Euston local on 2 August 1963. Later locomotives, including D5126

seen **(above)** passing Hilton Junction south of Perth with an empty stock train for Stirling in the early 1960s, were fitted with roof-mounted four-character headcode panels, and the front end was cleaned up by the removal of the original headcode discs and lowering of the tail lamps. The next batch of locomotives to be built, Nos D5151-D5232, were fitted with the more powerful 1,250hp Sulzer 6LDA28-B engine, as were all the subsequent batches Nos D5233-99 and Nos D7500-D7677. Later locomotives, like No D5282 pictured here **(below)** ambling past Kibworth on a down permanent way

20

train on 8 April 1968, were originally turned out in a smart two-tone green paint scheme; by this time the interconnecting doors in the cab front had been dispensed with, allowing a more pleasing full height centre window in the cab, while the horns were incorporated in the roof indicator housing.

When BR introduced their numerical classification system, the first 151 1,160hp locomotives became Class 24, while the remainder became Class 25, sub-divided into Classes 25/0, 25/1, 25/2 and 25/3 according to the variety of their electrical equipment. Now in overall blue livery and newly-allocated to the Western Region to replace withdrawn diesel-hydraulics, Class 25/2 No 7505 **(above left)** carefully brings a train of empty short wheelbase china-clay wagons bound for St Blazey into the east end of Par station on 1 September 1972. Equally at home on passenger or freight work, Class 25s were to the fore when a shortage of serviceable dmus in the Plymouth Division forced a temporary reversion to locomotive haulage of local passenger workings in the summer of 1976, and Class 25/2 No 25.223 here catches the evening sun as it hurries a scratch rake of stock past Dawlish Warren **(below left)** on the 19.30 Exeter-Paignton on 21 June. There were eventually 477 locomotives in the two classes until retirement of odd Class 24 locomotives began in 1969, and continued over the next few years, mainly due to accident damage. Withdrawal began in earnest in 1975, and most of Class 24 disappeared over the next two years, including latterly No 5113 seen **(above)** slowing for the token exchange at Garve with the lightly-loaded 13.30 Kyle of Lochalsh-Inverness freight on a wet 30 May 1972. One Class 24, No 24.032, has been preserved on the North Yorkshire Moors Railway and now sports the early two-tone green livery – which in fact it never carried in BR days – and its original number D5032, while sister locomotive No 24.061 has gone to the Research Centre at Derby and has been renumbered RDB 968007.
/D. Cross; Brian Stephenson; J.H. Cooper-Smith (2); G.F. Gillham (2); A. Williams

Another of the pilot scheme Type 2 designs to enjoy success was the Birmingham Railway Carriage and Wagon Co Bo-Bo first introduced in 1958. Powered by the same Sulzer 6LDA28 1,160hp engine as the Class 24, the first 'Birmingham Sulzers', Nos D5300-46, went to work on Great Northern Line suburban services, and thus almost new No D5304 is to be seen negotiating the station yard at Kings Cross **(above)** in Summer 1959. Like the BR Derby Sulzers, later batches of Birmingham-built locomotives, Nos D5347-D5415, were equipped with the more powerful 1,250hp Sulzer 6LDA 28-B engine and while some went to work in Scotland, others, like No D5407 pictured **(below)** passing Elstree with a lightweight pick-up freight, were allocated to Cricklewood Depot for Midland line duties. Over the years, more and more locomotives were transferred to Scottish Region depots, and now the entire class, still intact save for accident-damaged withdrawals, is concentrated at just four depots in Scotland. BR classified the first 1,160hp batch of locomotives as Class 26, and the later more powerful locomotives as Class 27 with the

push-pull fitted locomotives sub-divided into Class 27/1 (without electric heating) and 27/2 (with electric heating). Inverness-based Class 26 No 26.036, complete with small patrol snow ploughs **(above)** shunts vans at Kyle of Lochalsh on 27 May 1976, while push-pull fitted No 27.208 **(below)** leads a rake of six push-pull coaches and sister locomotive No 27.108 through Princes Street Gardens on the last stage of their journey into Edinburgh with the 14.00 from Glasgow on 27 April 1977. Although the recent influx of more modern, heavier locomotives has now somewhat reduced their monoply, Classes 24/25 and 26/27 dominated Highland line services for more than a decade in the 1960s and early 1970s, often double heading if necessary. Setting off from Inverness **(overleaf)** on a cloudy day in the early 1960s are No D5326 and Derby Sulzer No D5121 with a medium weight stopping train for Aviemore and Perth.
/J.B. Bucknell; B. Stephenson; B. Morrison; G.A. Watt; E. Treacy

5326

Charitably described at the time as 'not the most attractive of BR's new diesels', No D5700, the first of 20 unusual five-axled Type 2 locomotives built by Metropolitan Vickers, received a mixed reception when it made its debut in 1958 **(above).** Although the authorities were always careful to describe the unusual wheel arrangement as Co-Bo, rather than the more obvious but mirthful Bo-Co, many traditional railwaymen found it difficult to take a diesel with more wheels at one end than the other seriously, especially as it offered no real power advantage over other, lighter conventional Bo-Bo designs then also under construction. All 20 locomotives, Nos D5700-19, were originally allocated to the Midland Division of the LMR, and were put to work, often in pairs, on both main line passenger and express freight work, including the 'Condor' London-Glasgow overnight container train; whirring past Radlett on one of the former duties at the head of a St Pancras-Manchester express **(above right)** in Summer 1959 are D5717 and D5711. Soon, however, the Midland began to receive more powerful diesel locomotives, including 2,200hp 'Peak' class Type 4 locomotives, and the 1,200hp Co-Bos, with their sometimes

troublesome Crossley two-stroke 8-cylinder V8 engines, were banished to ex-Furness Railway metals in the far north-west, where they worked until the end of their days on both passenger and freight duties out of Barrow. Now with a yellow warning panel, and with a bowler-hatted inspector in the cab to see fair play, Tebay-based D5707 prepares to leave the ICI Tunstead works with a load of 19 bogie limestone hoppers on 14 June 1963 **(below left)** and the following summer is to be found waiting impatiently at Preston station **(below right)** for the signal to start with the 14.55 Preston-Barrow on 30 August 1964.

With 3ft 3in driving wheels, compared to the 3ft 7in or even 3ft 8in of their rivals, the MetroVick Co-Bos were fairly swift in acceleration, but nevertheless only just outlived the steam engines they had ostensibly come to replace, for the entire fleet of what would have been Class 28 if they had survived long enough were withdrawn from traffic in 1968, just 10 years after their initial introduction. Curiously, however, just one locomotive, the erstwhile No D5705, has survived as long again in Departmental stock, in use for experimental purposes as No TDB 968006. */BR; J.H.W. Kent; GEC; N.A. Machell*

Looking remarkably like the Class 22 diesel-hydraulic B-Bs from the same stable, the North British Type 2 diesel-electric Bo-Bos, introduced in 1959, were also originally fitted with virtually the same NBL/MAN 12-cylinder pressure charged 1,000hp engines. Although sent initially to work on the Eastern Region – No D6107 is seen **(above)** at Doncaster in the company of the prototype No D6100 early in their careers – the class subsequently gradually found their way to Scottish Region metals. In all, 58 locomotives, Nos D6100-57, were built, but again like the Class 22 diesel-hydraulics, later locomotives were fitted with an uprated 1,100hp version of the MAN engine; No D6138, seen heading north over the viaduct at Relly Mill **(below right)** with English Electric Type 4 No D259 on 12 February 1960, was the first of the uprated locomotives. In their Scottish habitat, the Class 29s were not popular because of their recurrent engine troubles, and in the mid-1960s a start was made on re-equipping some of the earlier locomotives

with Paxman 1,350hp engines, and by the beginning of 1968 when withdrawal of the remainder of the class began, 20 locomotives, Nos 6100-3/6-8/12-4/6/9/21/3/4/9/30/2/3/7, all from the original 1,000hp batch, had been re-engined. The rest of the class, including all the later 1,100hp locomotives, had gone by the end of the year, but the re-engined locomotives, now with their cab end doors sealed and sporting four-character headcode panels, soldiered on; No D6107, in blue livery, pulls away from Corrour **(below left)** on the last few yards of the climb to the summit of the West Highland line with the 06.00 Glasgow-Mallaig on 7 May 1968, while sister locomotives Nos 6112/32, both still in green livery, head a Grangemouth-Braehead oil train at Greenhill Junction, Falkirk, **(above right)** on what proved to be one of the last Class 29 turns on 2 November 1971.
/J.B. Bucknall; C.W.F. Bowman; D. Cross; I.S. Carr

D5500

20
D5507

On a wet mid-November day in 1957, No D5500, the first main line diesel locomotive to be delivered to the Eastern Region, worked its first revenue-earning duty, the 10.36 from Liverpool Street, seen **(above left)** arriving at Clacton. Built by Brush Traction at Loughborough and fitted with a Mirlees, Bickerton and Day 12-cylinder 1,250hp engine, the new locomotives weighed in at a fairly hefty 104 tons and were therefore carried on six-wheel bogies in an A1A-A1A wheel arrangement. The first 20 locomotives ,Nos D5500-19, were equipped with electro-magnetic control gear, and could therefore only work in multiple with other 'red spot' locomotives wired in a similar way. Subsequent locomotives, from No D5520 onwards, were fitted with electro-pneumatic control gear and were thus able to work with the vast majority of other BR diesel classes which have similar control gear and are coded 'blue star'. Although one of the first of the Type 2 designs to appear on the Modernisation scene, the 'Brushes' proved popular with both crews and maintenance staff, and construction continued apace over the next few years, 263 locomotives, Nos D5500-D5699 and D5800-62, eventually being built. Apart from the fitting of 1,365hp engines to locomotives from D5520 onwards, and the substitution of a roof-mounted four character headcode panel for the original headcode discs, there was little outward change in the appearance of the locomotives, all of which were at first allocated to the Eastern Region, for services on both the Great Eastern and Great Northern lines. Ten years after its introduction, and showing little outward sign of change apart from acquiring a yellow warning panel, No D5507 takes the North London line at Stratford **(below left)** with a mixed freight from Temple Mills on 29 October 1968, while later sister locomotive No D5692 threads the East Suffolk countryside between Westerfield and Bealings **(above right)** with the summer Saturday 10.50 Liverpool Street-Yarmouth South Town on 13 August 1966.

But whilst external changes in the mid-1960s may have been few, the Brush Type 2s were in fact at this time undergoing no less than a major heart transplant, for the entire class, including the first 20 locomotives, were re-engined between 1965 and 1969 with English Electric 12-cylinder 1,470hp engines, the originals, after some early promising upratings to 1,600hp and, in the case of D5835, to 2,000hp for a time, having subsequently proved troublesome. Under the BR classification scheme, the electro-magnetic control locomotives became Class 31/0 Nos 31.001-19 (No D5518 was fitted with electro-pneumatic control gear in 1970 and reclassified 31/1) while the remainder became Class 31/1 and were renumbered from 31.101 onwards, although those locomotives within this batch fitted with electric train heating equipment were classified 31/4 and numbered in a separate series from 31.401. Subsequently, additional locomotives have been similarly equipped and renumbered again from the 31.101 series to the 31.401 sequence.

The arrival of more modern motive power, the extension of electrification on the Great Eastern lines and, more recently, the Great Northern, has resulted in a gradual drift of Class 31 away from its traditional Eastern Region haunts to pastures new. The class is now regularly to be seen working further north up the East Coast main line – No 31.277 is seen heading south past Darlington **(above)** with a mixed freight on 13 June 1974, while sister locomotives Nos 31.113 and 31.232 power an up parcels train along the quadruple track section near Pilmoor on 10 April 1976 **(above right)** – as well as on the Western Region, working empty stock out of Paddington, and even as far west as Exeter, where the camera caught No 31.112 **(below right)** leaving St Davids with a morning train to Newton Abbot on 13 July 1976. The class also appear more regularly on inter-Regional trains, and in recent times have been the mainstay of the improved Portsmouth-Southampton-Salisbury-Bristol cross country services. Withdrawal of the first Class 31/0 locomotives began in 1976, but the class remains substantially intact, although many examples are now over 20 years old.
/B.R.; J.H. Cooper-Smith; G.R. Mortimer; B. Morrison (2); J.E. Oxley

0000

0000
31112

Although not the most numerous locomotives on BR, the Class 33 Bo-Bos are certainly among the most versatile and hard-working. Introduced in 1960 specifically for service on the Southern Region and therefore, uniquely among BR diesels, fitted with an SR-pattern two character headcode panel from the outset, this Birmingham Carriage and Wagon Co Type 3 design was basically an uprated version of the Class 27 Type 2 design from the same stable, with a Sulzer 8-cylinder 1,550hp engine. Nicknamed 'Cromptons' by the Southern men because of their Crompton-Parkinson traction equipment, the newcomers quickly proved to be versatile even among devout protagonists of electric traction; 98 locomotives were built, the last 12 with narrower bodies to 'Hastings Gauge' to enable their operation through the severly restricted tunnels on the Tonbridge-Hastings line. From the outset, the locomotives were put to work on inter-regional trains as well as domestic tasks, and were to be seen as far afield as the Great Northern line on cement trains, at Bromsgrove **(below left)**, as evidenced by No D6583 passing a string of Lickey bankers with a northbound Esso oil train on 18 June 1963, as well as on everyday cross-London inter-Regional freights, like the transfer freight for Norwood Yard seen easing through the reverse curves at Clapham Junction **(above left)** behind No D6581 on 31 August 1963. They seemed quite at home, too, piloting 'foreign' motive power; No D6556 enjoys a moment of glory **(above right)** as it leads 'West Country' Pacific No 34017 *Ilfracombe* over the single line away from Alton with the 'Bournemouth Belle' on 24 April 1966, diverted from the main line because of engineering works, while No 6544 joins forces with Type 3 diesel-hydraulic power in the form of Class 35 'Hymek' No 7045 **(below right)** as they accelerate away from Westbury on 17

B1

194

June 1972 on a Weymouth-Bristol working.

In readiness for the Bournemouth line electrification in 1967, 19 of the class were equipped with buck-eye couplings and multiple-unit control gear to enable them to work push-pull with the new TC trailer units over the non-electrified lines between Bournemouth and Weymouth, and also to work certain Salisbury line rush hour trains out of Waterloo without the need to run round or have a pilot locomotive at the London terminus. These locomotives, perhaps the most versatile on BR, regularly also work in multiple with SR electric units and the Class 73 electro-diesels. Under the BR numerical classification, the 'Cromptons' became Class 33, the basic locomotives Class 33/0 Nos 33.001-65, the push-pull fitted variety Class 33/1 Nos 33.101-19, and narrow-bodied Hastings gauge locomotives Class 33/2 Nos 33.201-12. Three locomotives have been lost as a result of accident damage, but otherwise the class continues to exhibit its remarkably catholic prowess. After the demise of the Class 42 'Warships' on the Waterloo-Exeter line, Class 33s took over this quite rigorous task, and No 33.023 is seen leaving Exeter St Davids **(preceding page)** with the 10.10 to Waterloo on 13 July 1976, while a few days later, on 18 July, sister No 33.036 was to be seen hurrying through Meopham under the watchful eye of a young enthusiast (**above**) with the return empty stock of a special train from Victoria to Farningham Road for the British Grand Prix at Brands Hatch. Exhibiting yet another aspect of its abilities **(above right)** is Class 33/1 No 33.119 propelling an instruction coach out of Clapham Yard on 18 September 1974, while the 'narrow body' look of Class 33/2 is exhibited by No 33.208 **(below right)** as it takes the West London line at Clapham Junction on 4 June 1975 with a train of coal empties from Wimbledon to the Western Region.

/B. Stephenson; A.A. Vickers; M. Pope; J.H. Sparkes; B. Morrison(3); R.I. Wallace

33 119

KH
33208

The Type 3 design for the Western Region, introduced in 1961, reflected Paddington's continuing penchant for diesel-hydraulic power and employed a Bristol-Siddeley/Maybach 1,700hp engine and a Stone-Maybach Mekydro hydraulic transmission; 101 locomotives, numbered D7000-D7100, were built by Beyer-Peacock and their outward appearance, which owed much to the attention of BRs Design Panel, was a marked improvement on the earlier WR hydraulic locomotive designs. Over the next few years the 'Hymeks' worked extensively over Western Region metals, although forays onto other Regions were comparatively rare: one disadvantage was that their unique control system precluded their working in multiple with other locomotive types, even those from the hydraulic stable. In the London area they were mainly seen on mixed traffic duties, such as the down van train seen **(right)** passing Old Oak Common on 10 September 1966 in the charge of D7065 which here still sports its original two-tone green livery, white cab surround and the raised cabside numerals which were later to present problems when, first, the 'D' prefix was dropped and, later, renumbering to conform with the five character TOPS computer system was contemplated. By now wearing blue livery, and with its 'D' prefix painted over as a gesture, No 7085 edges slowly into Cardiff General **(above)** with a train from Portsmouth on 1 October 1968, and meets Class 45 No D106 heading east on the through line with an up freight. With the shift in policy at Paddington in favour of diesel-electric traction, it became clear that the 'Hymeks', like their other hydraulic cousins, would not be among the longest-lived of BR diesels, and withdrawal duly began in 1971, continuing with such vehemence that by the end of 1972, only 21 locomotives remained. Whether because of their intended imminent demise, or because of the difficulty in amending the raised cab side numerals, the remaining 'Hymeks', although allocated Class 35, were not included in the general renumbering of 1973, and retained their original numbers as the class dwindled to 10 at 1974, a prelude to total withdrawal in the following year. However, no less than three of the class have been preserved, No 7017 by the Diesel and Electric Group on the West Somerset Railway, No 7018 at Didcot, and No 7029 at Swindon.
/C.T. Gifford; P.H. Groom

1F19
5

3A03

N
D6712

5T17
THE 300 TH
ENGLISH ELECTRIC
STANDARD TYPE 3 DIESEL ELECTRIC LOCOMOTIVE
FOR BRITISH RAILWAYS

Despite the rather dated look – high cabs and big bonnets were definitely passe when No D6700 first appeared in 1961 – the English Electric Type 3 Co-Co design quickly found favour with the operating men, who were looking for locomotives which were more powerful than the early Type 2s, yet not so cumbersome as the original Type 4s. The 'EE3s', as they became known, handsomely filled this gap with their 12-cylinder 1,750hp engines and 90mph performance, and sights such as that at the old Leeds Central **(above left)**, with No D6712 taking a breather with a Fairburn Class 4 2-6-4T in 1962, quickly became commonplace. By October 1965, English Electric were able to boast the construction of 'The 300th Standard Type 3 diesel-electric locomotive for British Railways', No D6999 **(below left)** and the locomotive is seen here on its first revenue-earning task with a block coal train for the Spencer Steelworks at Llanwern. Eventually, 309 locomotives were built, Nos D6700-99 and then D6600-8, although No D6983 was an early accident casualty. The first locomotives, like D6712, had rather messy front ends, with end doors in the nose, split, clumsy-looking headcode panels, and rather prominent grilles for the horns; but later examples like No D6947 hurrying a train of Presflos past Willesden North Junction **(above)** on the North London line on 2 June 1969, did away with the end doors, had a neater, single headcode panel, and removed the horns to a prominent position above the cab roof. Although the EE3s, now BR Class 37, are regular and reliable performers on the Eastern Region and in Scotland – No 6905 is seen **(overleaf, left)** in charge of a down freight on the West Coast main line near Abington on 6 June 1970 – it has been in the Bristol and South Wales areas that they have really been able to show their abilities, especially on the block coal and mineral trains that abound in the South Wales valleys. Double-heading is quite common, as with Nos 6886 and 6997 passing Bedminster Park, Bristol with a westbound fly-ash train on 21 May 1971 **(overleaf, top right)** and in more recent years triple-heading has been adopted for the hefty Port Talbot – Llanwern works ore trains. Leading one such 5,000hp-plus combination through Cardiff **(overleaf, below right)** on 24 October 1977 is No 37.202, its four-character headcode panel replaced with the now standard 'twin spot' warning panel.
/E. Treacy; GEC; J.H. Cooper-Smith(3); D.E. Canning

6B55

EMPRESS
VOYAGER
D210

D250

6B55

EMPRESS
VOYAGER
D210

D250

The first 'express passenger' Type 4 locomotive design to appear under the Modernisation Plan, perhaps not surprisingly in view of their close involvement with the LMS and Southern prototypes, was from English Electric and indeed, when No D200, the first locomotive, was turned out in May 1958 many commented on the similarities between the prototype designs and the newcomer. Weighing a hefty 133 tons and employing virtually the same English Electric 16 cylinder 2,000hp engine as No10203, the 'EE4s' had high cabs and long distinctive bonnets, with buffers mounted on the huge four-axle bogies rather than the locomotive mainframe. The first 10 locomotives went to work on the Eastern Region, but the next batch of 25 were sent to the London Midland Region, who from 1960 bestowed names from well known Cunard liners on their allocation – No D210 *Empress of Britain*, suitably spruced up with a fresh coat of paint and white buffers, poses for the camera **(above left)** at Euston after the naming ceremony on 12 May 1960. In all, 200 locomotives Nos D200-D399 were built by English Electric, and the class, with its distinctive turboblower whistle, provided the backbone of the first dieselised main line services on both the Eastern and London Midland Regions in the early 1960s; No D250 threads the outskirts of Leeds at Beeston with the up 'Queen of Scots' Pullman **(left)** in summer 1963, while over on the West Coast main line, No D328 on the down 'Caledonian' meets sister locomotive No D219 on the up 'Irish Mail' north of Rugby **(above)** on a warm August day in 1962. Like all the early Modernisation Plan diesels, the English Electric Type 4s were fitted with nose end doors to allow access between locomotives when running in multiple. In practice, however, the facility was little used, and the doors were subsequently sealed on earlier locomotives, and omitted altogether on later examples, allowing the split indicators seen on D328 to be replaced by the neater, central panel seen on D370 **(below)** as it pulls away from Wigan (North Western) with a morning Crewe-Glasgow parcels train on 12 May 1968.
/B.R.; E. Treacy; D. Wharton

With the advent of more modern motive power, and the extension of electric traction on the West Coast main line, the EE Type 4s, now BR Class 40, have found work further afield, and on rather more mundane freight duties – a task for which, it must be said, their considerable length and weight makes them less than ideally suited, the leading pony wheels in particular proving susceptible to derailment on sharply curved, badly aligned freight tracks. They still, however, find some passenger work; No 40.081 picks its way carefully into Dundee Tay Bridge station **(above)** with an Edinburgh-Aberdeen train on 7 December 1974, while the following summer, on 17 July, No 40.111 passes Arpley Junction, Warrington **(above right)** with a short coal train for Widnes while a Class 47 waits in the background with a westbound train of empty hopper wagons. Apart from the loss of No D322 in 1967 as a result of accident damage, the class remained intact until 1976, when withdrawal of some of the early examples began. But No 40.153 was still in full cry **(right)** as it hurried a mixed freight south down the East Coast main line near Aycliffe, north of Darlington, in July 1977.
/B. Morrison; P.D. Hawkins; R. Wildsmith

40 153

A50

The appearance of No D200 on the Eastern Region in 1958 was matched by the arrival on the Western Region of No D600 *Active* **(below)**, the first of its 'Warship' class main line diesel-hydraulic locomotives. Built by North British and powered by twin NBL/MAN 12-cylinder 1,000hp engines, the new locomotive weighed over 117 tons and was mounted on two six-wheel bogies, the middle axle of which was unpowered. Despite its brave name, *Active* suffered considerable teething troubles, and only four more locomotives, Nos D601-4, were built. But BR had not been idle at Swindon, and later in 1958, the works turned out the first of their own design of 'Warship' No D800 *Sir Brian Robertson*, a lighter B-B design, based on German Railways practice and employing two Bristol Siddeley-Maybach engines, each of 1,000hp, and Mekydro transmissions. In all, Swindon turned out 38 locomotives, Nos D800-32 and D866-70; those from D803 onwards were fitted with two uprated engines of 1,100hp each, while No D830 *Majestic* was fitted with two Paxman 1,200hp engines giving a total of 2,400hp. Meanwhile, North British adopted the Swindon design in preference to their own, and from 1960 turned out 33 locomotives, Nos D833-65, which were virtually identical externally to the Swindon-built variety, but instead employed an uprated 1,100hp version of the NBL/MAN engines used in their original 'Warship' design, and Voith transmissions. One of the first Swindon warships, No D803 *Albion* clatters through Box **(left)** on the climb to the tunnels with one of the hourly Weston-super Mare-Paddington trains in the summer of 1959, while one of the last, No D867 *Zenith* leads North British-built sister No D848 *Sultan* away from its birthplace **(above)** with a morning Paddington-Weston train on 23 June 1963. /*G.F. Heiron; M. Pope; C.P. Boocock*

All five original North British 'Warships' Nos D600-4, together with the first three 2,000hp Swindon-built locomotives Nos D800-2 – which could not work in multiple with the remainder of the class – were withdrawn in 1968, and the sole Paxman-engined locomotive No D830 followed in 1969, but the rest remained in front line service until 1971, when withdrawal began; all the North British locomotives had gone by the end of that year, but the last of the Swindon variety remained in traffic until mid-1972. Ironically, in view of the fact that they were one of the few early diesel designs not to feature end interconnecting doors, the 'Warships' were often to be seen working in tandem, especially on West of England trains. One such pairing approaching journey's end **(above)** is No 803 *Albion* – now with a four character headcode panel – and No 814 *Dragon* as they bring the up 'Cornish Riviera' into Paddington on 26 July 1969. Looking rather stained, but clearly still in business, No 825 *Intrepid* coasts down Dainton bank towards Totnes **(right)** with a down special on 6 August 1971. The last of the 'Warships', No D870 *Zulu* differed from the remainder in having a large, Western-style air intake mounted above the cab, well illustrated in this comparison with the then still almost new No D1047 *Western Lord* at Swindon works in May 1963. **(below)**/*J.H. Cooper-Smith* (2); *BR*

1Z48

The English Electric Type 4s did not retain their reputation as the most powerful – or the heaviest – diesel-electric locomotives on BR for long, because in 1959 the first of BRs own Type 4 design appeared in the shape of 'Peak' class 1Co-Co1 No D1 *Scafell Pike*. Similar in many ways to the EE4s, and again revealing the obvious parentage of the LMS prototypes Nos 10000/1, the first 10 'Peaks' Nos D1-10 were fitted with 2,300hp 12-cylinder Sulzer engines and weighed over 133 tons. In 1960 No D11 appeared, unnamed as was now the policy, and fitted with a more powerful 2,500hp engine; it proved to be the first of 183 locomotives, Nos D11-193, which were turned out over the next few years and mainly put to work on Midland line services from St Pancras, on north and west services, and in the then North Eastern Region. Locomotives from D138 onwards had Brush rather than Crompton Parkinson traction motors, as well as the dubious privilege of being, at 138 tons, the heaviest diesel locomotives on BR, a record that still stands today. Although the avowed Beeching line was not to encourage the cult of the personality with such quaint ideas as names for locomotives, over the years almost 30 of the class have acquired names, mostly of military origin and some the same as those carried by withdrawn 'Royal Scot' class steam locomotives. Under the BR classification scheme, Nos 1-10 became Class 44, Nos 11-137 Class 45, and Nos 138-93 Class 46; Classes 44 and 46 were simply renumbered in sequence, but those in Class 45 were subdivided

into those with dual steam and electric heating, Class 45/0 Nos 45.001-77, and those with electric train heating only, Class 45/1 Nos 45.101-50. They were mainly renumbered as they were overhauled, and the present numbers give little clue to their original sequence. The first 'Peaks' began their lives on the West Coast main line – No D7 *Ingleborough* is pictured here **(above left)** south of Berkhamsted on 4 November 1961 with the up 'Ulster Express' (the headboard for which must surely have restricted the drivers' field of vision) – but in more recent years, all 10 Class 44s have been based at Toton on the Midland line and it is in Toton Yard that Nos 44.002 *Helvellyn*, 44.010 *Tryfan*, 44.003 *Skiddaw* and 44.008 *Penyghent* were to be seen **(below right)** resting between duties on 31 August 1975, before the demise of the class began in 1976. Classes 45 and 46, however, soldier on and, like Class 40, find themselves on an increasingly varied diet of duties. Also like Class 40 has been the progression from the original disc-laden front end of the first 'Peaks', through the 'twin box' indicator phase seen on NoD93 **(below left)** departing from Gloucester with the northbound 'Devonian' on 7 July 1961, to the tidier-looking central display to which No 36 has been modified in this September 1974 view **(above right)** as it trundles an inter-regional freight off the West London line and under Clapham Junction 'A' signalbox to reach the Windsor lines.
/J.C. Beckett; C.P. Walker; B. Morrison(2)

Today, despite the introduction of newer locomotives, Classes 45 and 46 continue to provide front-line motive power for the Midland and North and West lines; in this busy May 1977 scene at Sheffield, Class 46 No 46.017 waits to depart for Leeds with an early morning train from Gloucester, while nearer the camera eth-fitted No 45.136 waits to take out the empty Mark 2 air conditioned stock of an earlier arrival from St Pancras./*A. Wynn*

1A03
D9001
D1505
1E04

SHEFFIELD MIDLAND
SHEFFIELD MIDLAND
Sheffield

Introduced in 1962 and looking (and sounding!) very much like the Birmingham Railway Carriage and Wagon Co prototype No D0260 *Lion*, and with the same Sulzer 12-cylinder 2,750hp engine, the Brush Type 4s have since established themselves as the workhorses of BRs diesel fleet. Described by one railwayman as the Stanier Class 5 of the diesel era, the 'Brushes' appear equally at home on express passenger or heavy freight work, and are to be found undertaking both tasks with equanimity on all regions of BR. In design, they were a very real advance on other classes only a few years older; the cab design was a breakthrough compared with the earlier Type 4s or even the much-vaunted 'Deltics', themselves only a year older, as seen in the view of D1505 and D9001 *St Paddy* **(above left)** at the buffer stops at Kings Cross on 5 October 1963, while the provision of more power on a lighter, more versatile Co-Co chassis quickly proved an advantage. Over the next few years no fewer than 512 locomotives, Nos D1500-1999 and D1100-11, were built by Brush and turned out in the attractive two-tone green livery that is still worn by No 1631 as it heads beneath an array of semaphores for the tunnels north of Sheffield **(left)** with the down 'Thames-Clyde Express' on the 16 June 1970, and indeed, if rather shabbily, by 1666 *Odin*, one of the 17 locomotives named by the Western Region, as it, too picks its way through a forest of signals into the platforms at Swansea **(above)** with the 08.00 from Paddington on 1 June 1971.
/B. Stephenson; D.L. Percival; J. H. Cooper-Smith

The 'Brushes' became Class 47 under BRs classification scheme. With renumbering in 1973, they were split into sub-classes – 47/0 for those fitted with steam-heating boilers, 47/3 for those with no train heating equipment at all, and 47/4 for those fitted with dual or electric train heating equipment only. As might be expected, there has been some replacement of steam heating boilers with the equipment, and consequent renumbering from 47/0 series numbers to the 47/4 series, while in 1975 No 47.046 was equipped with a GEC Diesels 16-cylinder 3,520hp engine, reclassified 47/6 and renumbered 47.601 (now 47.901), proving to be the prototype for the subsequent Class 56 diesels. Apart from accident damage, which has written off no less than three Class 47s over the years, the entire class remains in traffic right across BR. Representing the increasing number of 47/4 eth-fitted locomotives are No 47.458 **(below)** setting out across the Tay Bridge with the 18.15 Dundee-Edinburgh train on 3 September 1977, and at the other end of the line, No 47.546 **(below right)** arriving at Kings Cross on 12 June 1975 with 'The Newcastle Executive' express, while one of the Class 47/3s (not fitted with heating equipment and thus restricted to freight work in the winter months) is No 47.325 **(above right)** wheeling a lengthy southbound train of coal hoppers through the now disused southerly platforms at Nottingham Midland on 10 July 1975. In recent months, 12 locomotives on the Scottish Region have undergone a further metamorphosis to emerge as Class 47/7 Nos 47.701-12. All are named and equipped with push-pull control equipment for work on the new high-speed service between Edinburgh and Glasgow. */ L. A. Nixon; P. D. Hawkins; B. Morrison*

5
6T55

8
1
Inter-City

The early 1960s saw a minor spate of Co-Co diesel prototypes from various manufacturers for which BR provided facilities for testing, both experimentally and in everyday traffic conditions, but which remained the property of the owners and were not therefore included in BR stock. First to appear, in 1961, was the Brush *Falcon*, with the rather odd number D0280 and powered by two Maybach V-type engines of 1,400hp. Finished in a distinctive and not unattractive two-tone livery, *Falcon* soon settled down to routine work on the East Coast main line, one of its regular duties for a time being the 'Master Cutler' and 'Sheffield Pullman' trains, and it is at the head of the latter as it swings sharply away from the main line at Retford **(above left)** that *Falcon* is seen on the down working on 24 April 1962. In that year, the second of the prototypes, rather confusingly numbered D0260 and named *Lion*, was turned out by the Birmingham Railway Carriage & Wagon Co. A rather impressive locomotive but finished in an unlikely and certainly totally impractical all-over white livery – right down to buffers, couplings and bogies **(below right)** – it was powered by the same Sulzer 12-cylinder 2,750hp engine as the Brush Type 4s

introduced that year, and indeed revealed a marked similarity to those locomotives in both cab and front end design. As well as some impressive trials on the Lickey incline, *Lion*, like *Falcon*, put in some everyday work on East Coast main line duties, and is seen, already looking somewhat grubby **(above right)** accelerating through Beeston Junction on the outskirts of Leeds with the up 'Yorkshire Pullman' on a fine day in 1963. But whereas *Lion*'s career on BR spanned less than a couple of years, *Falcon* continued to work in traffic, and in 1970 was taken into stock as Class 53 No 1200. However, although it was the only other BR diesel outside Classes 50 and 55 to be capable of 100mph operation, it spent most of its latter years working freight in South Wales from Newport Ebbw Junction depot, and it is here that No 1200 – it was not renumbered in 1973 – is seen arriving with a short down mixed freight **(below left)** on 24 April 1975, shortly before its final demise only a matter of weeks later.
/J. Cupit; P.D. Hawkins; E. Treacy; GEC

1A40
DP2

A
B
C
D
1G60
DP2

Another prototype to take to BR metals in 1962 was the English Electric Diesel Prototype Two, hence numbered DP2; one presumes that the prototype 'Deltic' was reckoned to have been DP1. Built on the same assembly line and using the same jigs as the production Type 5 'Deltics', No DP2 was externally virtually their twin, but employed a conventional English Electric 16-cylinder 2,700hp engine. At first DP2 was put through its paces on the London Midland Region and is pictured here coming off the Runcorn Bridge **(above left)** with an up Liverpool train in the early days of its trials, but before long it was transferred to the Eastern Region to join its 'Deltic' half-sisters, one of which idles in the background **(below left)** as DP2, now even painted in look-alike 'Deltic' two-tone green livery, departs from Kings Cross with a down Pullman train in August 1965. On the East Coast main line, DP2 put up some fine performances until its career came to an abrupt and unfortunate end on 31 July 1967 when it collided at speed with a derailed cement train near Thirsk and was damaged beyond repair. But even as DP2 bowed out, yet another prototype locomotive was nearing completion. For many people the most stylish diesel locomotive ever to take to BR metals, and even today certainly the most powerful, the Brush/Hawker Siddeley HS 4000 *Kestrel* was a 4,000hp Sulzer-powered machine with 125mph potential. Introduced in 1968, it entered public service in October the following year and is seen at Kings Cross **(above)** in its striking chocolate and yellow livery on one of its first revenue-earning workings at the head of the 16.20 to York. Despite some impressive performances, however, the engineers expressed concern at the effect of its 126-ton weight on their track – although it is worth noting that this is no more than today's Class 56 – and *Kestrel* retired to Brush Electrical at Loughborough in 1971 to be regauged for sale to the Soviet Union. */BR(2); Hawker Siddeley*

1S57

By the time DP2 met its unfortunate end in 1967, BR had been sufficiently convinced of its prowess to agree to hire 50 Type 4 locomotives from English Electric with the same 16-cylinder 2,700hp engine, but with a more modern Brush-type cab layout. Numbered D400-49, the new locomotives were introduced directly into front line service, often in tandem, on the accelerated Anglo-Scottish trains on the then unelectrified section of the West Coast main line north of Crewe, and it is on such duty that Nos 409 and 408 pass Springs Branch No 2 signalbox **(this page)** as they come into Wigan on the down 'Royal Scot' on 13 March 1971.

Electrification works brought inevitable disruption and delay to West Coast route Anglo-Scottish services in the early 1970s, and the new locomotives, now BR Class 50, found themselves regularly diverted to other routes and needing all their power to keep within recovery margins. Diverted to the ex-Glasgow and South Western Route via Kilmarnock and Dumfries because of Sunday engineering work on the Caledonian line, Nos 422 and 431 climb round the curves on the approach to Drumlanrig Tunnel **(overleaf, left)** on 21 May 1972 with a morning Glasgow-Euston express. With the completion of electrification to Glasgow in 1974, most of the Class 50s were transferred to the Western Region to replace ageing diesel-hydraulics on South Wales and West of England trains. With a train of Mk 2 air-conditioned stock in tow, No 50.049 emerges into the sunlight from Parsons Tunnel and skirts the sea wall near Teignmouth **(overleaf, top right)** as it heads for Plymouth with the 10.30 from Paddington on 15 September 1977. Late in 1977, BR reversed its earlier policy of not naming its main line express locomotives and the entire Class 50 was chosen for naming. The Western Region set about this task with a will, re-using some 'Warship' names, and both 50.010 *Monarch* and 50.048 *Dauntless* had received their smart new nameplates on 18 March 1978 as they wait at Derby Station **(overleaf, below right)** with a railtour special from Paddington to Matlock.
/J.H. Cooper-Smith(2); H.W. Cater; N.E. Preedy

Although the 'Warships' were well equal to most of the passenger duties inherited from steam days, like most of the first generation of 2,000hp-plus Type 4s, they did not have the reserves of power necessary for the longer, heavier and faster trains required of the diesel era, and the Western Region was forced to use them in tandem – a most inefficient and wasteful form of motive power – for speed on its crack expresses, and for extra power over the South Devon banks. The need was for a more powerful, six-axle locomotive, and in 1961 the first of the 'second generation' Type 4s appeared in the rather handsome form of 'Western 'class C-C No D1000 *Western Enterprise*. Built by BR and powered by two Maybach 1,350hp engines with Voith transmissions, the new locomotives, of which 74 were built over the next two years, immediately showed that they had the additional power necessary for the diesel age and, unlike the 'Warships', were rarely seen in tandem. And it was not only in terms of power that the 'Westerns' were superior to the 'Warships', for their rakish design revealed the handiwork of BR's industrial design team, the cab in particular being a great advance on the weak design of the 'Warships'. There were experiments with colour, too; No D1000 *Western Enterprise*, seen passing Canton shed **(above right)** on its way out of Cardiff on 13 August 1963 with the down 'Pembroke Coast Express', was originally finished in 'desert sand' livery, while subsequent locomotives appeared in shades of green, maroon and even golden ochre. Later locomotives from D1035 onwards were built at Crewe and originally painted green, but maroon was subsequently adopted as the 'standard' livery for the entire class. All were given names with a 'Western' prefix, and the class dominated Western Region express passenger work for the next decade. Maroon-

liveried No D1039 *Western King* heads an up Cardiff-Paddington service through a frosty Sonning Cutting on 8 March 1969 **(above left)** while blue painted No 1001 *Western Pathfinder* growls up to Dainton Summit **(overleaf)** with the 8.30 Paddington-Penzance on 6 August 1971. Allocated Class 52 in the BR classification scheme, the 'Westerns' were not renumbered in 1973, presumably because of the high cost of replacing their individual cast numberplates, although the 'D' prefix was painted out when it was dropped in 1968. With the trend away from hydraulic transmission in the 1970s, it was clear that the 'Westerns' would have to go in the name of standardisation, and their demise began in 1973 with the withdrawal of about 10 locomotives. However, despite the arrival of Class 50s displaced from the London Midland Region by electrification and, later, a whole fleet of HSTs, the 'Westerns' lingered on until 1977, albeit sometimes on less demanding duties. A fine Sunday evening in June 1976 finds No 1068 *Western Reliance* standing in Goodrington carriage sidings with a return excursion **(below left)**, while Nos 46.011 and 1013 *Western Ranger* arrive light to take up later workings. The 'Western' class has always been popular with enthusiasts, and their final weeks in service in early 1977 were marked by an unprecedented number of special 'farewell' trips. One of the class, No 1023 *Western Fusilier* is to be preserved, and is seen in unfamiliar country **(below right)** coasting into Leeds past the Freightliner depot at Stourton with the 'Western Finale' special from Exeter to York on 12 February 1977.
/G.P. Cooper; M.S. Wilkins; A.J. Wheeler; L.A. Nixon; J.H. Cooper-Smith

1B25

DELTIC
CANADIAN
TRADE
MISSION

1A35

Even as the Modernisation Plan was being announced in 1955, with its promises of widespread dieselisation, English Electric were busy building their prototype high horsepower Co-Co locomotive *Deltic* for experimental use on the East and West Coast main lines. Unlike the first LMS and SR prototypes, or indeed any of the first 'pilot scheme' locomotives that appeared in the next few years, all of which employed conventional diesel engines of various sizes and makes, *Deltic* was fitted with two high-speed 18-cylinder lightweight Napier 'Deltic 'engines of 1,650hp apiece, the design of which was derived from naval practice. The result was a high-speed 3,300hp locomotive weighing 106 tons – a considerable achievement compared to the first 2,000hp BR Type 4s, which tipped the scales at over 130 tons, and which it actually predated. The *Deltic* underwent intensive and prolonged test, on both special and service trains on both the Eastern and London Midland Regions, and one task during its spell on the latter was to bring a Canadian Trade Mission special from Glasgow to London. This view of the prototype departing from a dark and wet Glasgow Central **(above left)** clearly shows the rather dated styling which belied the actual performance of the locomotive. Five years of intensive running, in which time *Deltic* covered more than 450,000 miles, convinced the Eastern and Scottish Regions that this was what was needed to improve services on the East Coast Route, and No D9000, the first of 22 production locomotives, appeared in 1961, and is seen approaching Finsbury Park **(below left)** with the up 'Flying Scotsman' on 5 August 1961. Apart from exterior styling improvements, including a pleasing two-tone green livery with white cab surrounds, the production 'Deltics' were very much like the prototype, although they weighed a little less at 102 tons. Meanwhile, the prototype 'Deltic' had been retired from active service in 1960, and after complete refurbishment at English Electric's Vulcan Foundry works, was presented to the Science Museum in London. Resplendent in a new coat of blue paint *Deltic* is pictured here **(below)** at Rugby on its way south to its new home on 23 April 1963 in the charge of new English Electric Type 3 No D6822.

On the East Coast Route the arrival of the 'Deltics,' with their 100mph capability, enabled impressive improvements to timetabling, and over the years, as further stretches of track were brought up to 100mph standard, services from London to Yorkshire, the North East and Scotland were progressively accelerated. One such service was the 'Flying Scotsman', a regular 'Deltic' working until the introduction of HSTs, seen leaving Edinburgh Waverley **(overleaf)** in the mid-1960s in the charge of No D9009 *Alycidon./BR(2); C.P. Boocock; E. Treacy*

1A35
THE
FLYING
SCOTSMAN

D9009

D9020